Portal

Joyce Jenkins

Pennywhistle Press
Santa Fe
1993

Poems from this collection have previously appeared in the following publications: *Berkeley Poetry Review*, John F. Kennedy University's *Tunnel Road 2*, *The Bisbee Observer*, and *ZYZZYVA*. "Manifesto" was published as a broadside by Robert Schneck.

Cover photograph by Christopher Felver
Typography by Black Mesa Productions, Inc., Santa Fe
Cover design by The Groot Organization, San Francisco

Printed in the United States of America
by Publishers Press, Salt Lake City

ISBN: 0-938631-18-7

For additional copies, address orders to: Harbinger House
P.O. Box 42948
Tucson, AZ 85733-2948
(602) 326-9595
FAX 326-8684

Note: Poems with the following mark: ∿
at the bottom of the page are continued on the next page.

Contents

Introduction

"And I have been influenced by the voices / of my generation / fragmented, in pieces, / whining in the tin ear of history / like bones rattling in a cup, / like luck, / like the worst day you / ever had . . ." This is Joyce Jenkins speaking, harder, more visceral that one might have expected knowing her; her gentleness. She manages the sounds of grief and loss, but from a distance, with an uncanny detachment:

> "The train station
> where you would not help me
> the light streamed through the high glass panes
> where you would not help me find the train
> the roof a great mosaic refracting ribbons
> > forever
> light for a thousand painters
> each facet a . . . jewel of heaven."

Jenkins, in the middle of her life, having lived for poetry, as she has said; having suffered and endured, she is without bitterness. Instead she has a witty fatalism: "The Angel of Beauty / plays with matches ..." And we all inhabit that beautiful, burning house of the world.

But life has not diminished her joyous energy, her playfulness. It's a rare combination: the playfulness of a very young girl, the wry wisdom of an old woman. It is emblematic in her childlike cheeks, her prematurely graying hair. We have loved her for her simplicity, but her poems show a complex nature we had hardly guessed. "This is a song about falling . . . This is a dance about dying . . . This is a map of the soul. You / will need a flashlight, a / miner's hat, a caged canary, / and one of those / thick coiled ropes."

This slender book is all the proof we need that she possessed all the required equipment: the light, the hat, the bird, the rope—with which she can scale heights or plumb depths, from the serene super-ego to the shadowy psyche. All we ask of her, then, is that she give a little less of herself to the rest of us, we poets, and be more diligent in selfishness (we can give lessons!) so that her next book will be fuller and fatter, that we may re-joice in Joyce.

Carolyn Kizer

[v]

MANIFESTO

I am a generic item.
This brand is cheaper
and will clean anything.
Wavy little anemone, reaching up—
I'm not quite sly enough
to be a 'good' woman.
Mother doesn't know

I battered my thighs in the car.
We were on the way home
from delivering   your mother.
"I don't want to be a woman—
I don't want to be a—" choked
up, a curse, from my throat.

You are your mother's son.
So with little chisel sparking,
I turned myself to stone.

I am *faux* not real
though father   thought I was
and mother wasn't—

It was a lie. Sweet flattery forged
of me a sword and swung me smart
to slash my mother's limbs.

A bruised sponge has memory but no tongue.
Tangled in kelp we struggled
salt and blood filled our plates.

I had nothing but a memory
Detached   I watched it rise

~

The red light slowly developed
what was there, the image like an old Southern

tintype, the image materializing glossy and sharp
on the paper   under water   in the dark.

I don't want to be a woman
but then the dream of the companion returns—
I don't want to be a woman
but lean towards the male
in squashed hat and Western shirt
chauffeur cap and tweedy suit

I am a generic item   I see

baseball caps and ripped open tees

I don't want to be a woman

But I want them to enter me
like the doorway to the moon
I want them to enter but
the huge rock rolls in front of the cave
and the hunger is trapped, can't escape

runs in the tissues but not sweetly
it races a loop of vein and vessel
rein in, rein in
o please
take the ache away

and I say the vagina isn't a tomb
but they don't believe me or the
witness of my blood.   ~

So I learned long ago
don't try for what you want
let them go
you can never have them
anyway   I don't want to
I never wanted to
be a woman
filled with this image of a goddess
and no way to touch her
in this life—

I am marching with a tiny
candle   in the rain
I push through carnaval   the crowds
my little ones are hungry   dust
devils in the abandoned
sheep run   the Latin jungle
foliage   snaps back
in my face. They are Rastafarian.
They are Czech. They are hungry
They are innocent. Mother
is ill or gone.

I am all that's left.
There is nothing left to sell.

I am commonly available   not protected
by trademark   descriptive of an entire
group or class. This brand
is cheaper and will clean
and will clean
and will clean
anything

just as well.

ANTHEM

All I want is to write poems!
Unrealistic action—
Unjustified life!

I don't care about direction. I love
my past. The future a white tiled

hall, no color, everything washed
w/ white. It doesn't have a temperature, no
sun or wind, no falling leaves or
seedlings, just white
sitting blindly, white shining cautiously, white

wandering abt/ wondering where it is.
                                        I
                                have no
colors on, my orange has gone white, my blue
has gone white. Even the silver on my wrist

has gone white. I can see
the whites of its eyes gleam

whitely. It is blind. We are

all blind. Trying to get a prescription for
    lenses, trying to press out of dust from
                        the floor/ *lenses*
                        to SEE with/

DISCOVERY

Let's take this cool and light.
The 'voice', my voice, but perhaps yours, resonates
from a particular place, tremor pool of the brain.
That is to say, the body, but also its less physical webs,
such as soul arc, aura. The point is midway, in a clearing.
It is night and the snow is incandescent.
To say this is to say a puzzle.
The 'voice' is authoritative
but not low, not mundane, and not vibrationally low.
The voice is not conscious of its act.
It is simple articulation: out-of-sync tongue
earnestly dubbing the undermind's script.
In the dark, the upheld signing hand
cannot own its deep perceptions,
can swim in its burning, freezing seas
only in sleep. There is
no dialogue, only the breeze over rippling tides
non-verbal call and response
self to self without consciousness of self,
and so with no lack of poise or balance.

Through the glittery night
the determined snowflake glides
crazy pinball
pings softly between the legs of the moon
swirls the silvery orchard
low bell stroke far away, dark tower on the horizon
luminous
luminous
tremulous quake at the red hot center
where ever you are
opening your mouth
to speak

True pitch, celestial chime
tuning fork quiver
wild spitfire
nerve to the heart.

(YOU WILL NEED A FLASHLIGHT)

There is a fear of heights,
the start in the night,
the step off a cliff
so steep there is no bottom,
just flashing legs
and arms with no bundles.
This is a song about falling,
and the words are a whistle
of last air from lung.

This is a dance about dying,
only here there are no
swans, just murky waters—
faces without mouths. This

is like one of those movies
about prize-fighting, leukemia,
or Marilyn Monroe. This is
the final pan to the smoke
ring, the bar sink; what
the maid left behind. This
is a map of the soul. You

will need a flashlight, a
miner's hat, a caged canary
and one of those
thick coiled ropes.

TO LOVE THE ARSONIST

Poor
cowboy, he was riding
the range cruising
old snowdrifts looking
for angels. Somewhere
an ember.

It was in his heart,
his ears, a warm
thump. It was she, it was
the photograph he'd
had for years. He
kept her framed on
the mantle, warm. One
day the memory revived,
sat up, stepped out,
breathed: "Cowboy—"
the fire flaming below.

She put her hands on his
shoulders, called him
golden honey, then snapped his

ruddy neck like a branch.
That was what they had together,
flushed cheeks, charred
elbows, surprise.

THE LAST COWBOY

It seems far off, but it's not that far off,
all that bread, all that butter. Angelboyfriend
take off your shirt, sit beside me a while on
this nice swing seat. Come listen to the truth
as it was observed one summer day, we had so much—
wine in the fridge, ribs, and hay, Oh angel—
look up at the sky, it's Venus, what we trembled
to touch, how my fingers grazed—
that arm those lips that cheek. I didn't want to
move out of that hallway, me more romantic than
you against the wall. You have a better memory,
always did, is that why you could take it or leave
it, my lips' purse, that table leg dug in my thigh?
When she captured your look, were you just standing
to go, suddenly tired of games? Still, we were
children. You didn't know what sinister thing
made you afraid, it was dim evening—Electricity
danced the abyss between us, the vast canyon I
mooned over you. Angelboy, you wanted, grown-up,
to be a cowboy. But lately, nobody is what
you are, riding an empty plain.

PIANO MAN

Friday night. Beautiful jazz piano at Picante's. Two people in the room. Three grubby skateboarders and several ticket holders waiting for their food in the next. The music, simple, yet impossibly lovely, impossibly complicated, pours out of the shiny black spinet. The piano player notices me listening. He can hear me listening. He turns his head slightly to look. I look away to avoid eye contact because the music is impossibly intimate. How can I tell him that it's okay that no one but me hears? That I will walk out and down Sixth Street and he will be alone but that he must not stop playing? That he is not alone as long as he sounds? That he means as long as he sounds? That he cannot stop playing. He must not.

POWER

A tiny bat could terrify a bull
by fording the twisted channels
of its memory, possessing it
with demon voices, a serpent's
tongue, the perfume of rotten
mango in a Mexican marketplace.
Power can make us loose, make us
swagger. When we aren't quite *there*
we sense it, sitting in cars, talking—
It numbs us.
Strangers begin to pass,
peripheral shrubs.
When they ask for nothing
we are relieved. A man strides
behind me, pounding his feet.
Am I strong enough? Could I fight?
Without turning I read the sky.
The horizon
is the stage. Splendor
consumes itself. A star steps out.
The Angel of Beauty
plays with matches. Her *aria*
is aggression. The sunset
smolders. I am breathing
hard. Power,
electrical,
telescopes my legs. They are pistons
and I slam them home. They are
pistons and the puny streetlights
streak. I push
out. The *a capella* night.

SUICIDE NOTE

You set your leg on the sill—
your heart a sliver halfway out.
I hear "This is all yours now—"
The window shimmers   a door to you
as you sail past, five
stories. A hawk's beak emerges
from the temple of your skull.
Elbows flap. Your pigeon
bones so gaunt you almost

float you almost fly.
The grass is still screaming

the screaming grass
the no sound scream

the silent street.
You finally made

contact.

THE EVIDENCE

for Telegraph Avenue

A woman swung out ahead of me,
trailing conchshell, tuberose, clove.
I never expect the delicate
on this avenue at noon. But there
I was, and there she went;
an overwrought abundance,
like too many ripe zucchini
or a sudden house of gold.

JOURNEY FROM AVIGNON

I understand now
the long dim nights
the days without myself,
no company
worth any time.
I understand the death of
self, of the moment, the loss
of the moment out
the moving train window,
remembering Belgium and being
afraid of the green plowed fields,
of the foreign children with notes
from their teachers in an
undecipherable hand,
afraid of the unknown tongue
unfolding in their throats
like mysterious toads.
Afraid of the children
with their powers of seduction,
angelic chords.
The train station
where you would not help me
the light streamed through the high glass panes
where you would not help me find the train
the roof a great mosaic refracting ribbons forever
light for a thousand painters
each facet a canvas, jewel of heaven.
Time languishes here,
and I mourn the strokes —
painter's time
the colors of the chapel
the virgin's shawl, blue
in the basement of the cathedral
a cathedral to mass

~

masses of roses
the great rose window
riding waves of wheat
the linen wraps of the relics
all decay   the metallic taste

of fork lying under the *nouvelle* meal.
Here in France, in Chartres
so far from our births
on this small earth,
I understand now

dust   gone popes
ancient, walled Avignon
monasteries plundered, split
little clay figures wrapped
in glorious nativity
brass beads, crumbling museums.

I understand now how the light
distilled your face when you lost
the keys to our hotel room

and you made me go back, look under the bed,
talk pidgin *français* with the amused *concierge*.
You made me speak in a tongue not mine
while the sun came through panes
in muddy ribbons, washing my soul

I understood. Compacted your face,
made it small like the earth
upside down in my pupils.
Made you an octagonal living moment

A single tile
to sit on the roof
to finish the job

on our world.

LOVE SONG

While I was with you I rubbed oils and lotions all over my skin. My hair became soft. I felt light. I noticed myself. I felt cared for. I noticed myself. I felt light. I felt the light. I felt you with me. You were with me. You were light. You were solid, but not too heavy. You cut the right shape out of the room. You were soft. You were solid. You were right.

GUAVAS

I suck pink juice
around in my mouth
and taste the yellow rind.
I do all my profoundest
thinking
lying on my side
car keys cupped in hand
like figs
like soft leathery
scrotum

"I got the whole world
in my hands."

BITTER LEMONS

Remember the Temple, its endless colonnade,
The bitter lemons printed with your teeth?
—Gérard de Nerval
(translated by Peter Jay)

Teeth dart, the biting
bared pearls graze the neckline
slip over pores
hands swirling over sweaty
marble   smooth
like the lemon
pungent
like the lemon
sexy
acrid
swift
sweet
like the lemon
teeth bite
sexy
sweet
oily
acid
lemon

oh.

All sweaty
the sweet then
the bitter
hair smells so spicy—

But when it burns?

•   ~

Under the jasmine
the white lemon rinds
photo-etch handprints
on his naked torso—acerbic
on the dusty desk, redwood
the color of nipples

and the teeth? printing?

Pearls glow yellow
like fire
like transformation

Hands pour sand
sand pours glass
blowing blue flame

Japanese fishing floats
blue glass globes
wash on to shore.

•

Running through the thistle
my little girl, excited
by the heavy-laden tree
tugs on the green
tough
lemons.

HAWAII SPEAK

O Goddess
of the burning stones
Let awe possess me.
　　　　　—prayer to Pele

You make poi-dogs bark, your leaves snap.
Fingers jump on your rough bones of coral.
Heart veiled in adolescent steam
you don't need to see, you
know yourself to be fire.
I can feel it
in your night face, Haleakala, the
white rain water
falling on petals of flame, the
road in your palm a knife thrown
through the jungle.
To Maui I went for mangoes,
pink guavas,
hands full of sand.
To you Big Island belong
terrible orchids
warrior footprints
and magma   magma   magma.

THIS SMALL EARTH

This small earth is the body
of the goddess.
Breasts like two rosy pippins
in a brawny hand.

PHOTOGRAPH

Mary, my mother, standing with her arm
about her friend all
blessed with white, white nylons,
white shoes, white nursing bib.
They are students with perky sleeves.
Their rubber soles squeak.
The darlings,
shaded
by the shadow
of the camera man, his
shoulders a stain
on the white light ground—

O mother. You saw
him coming,
but you were too honest
to move.

IN THE SPRING, THE DELICATE VIOLETS

In the spring, the delicate violets
are a value hard to fathom,
beyond the ken of a living look
or the keen of a swinging hoe. On the curved hill,
my mother loves. In summer,
surrounded by her vegetables, glorious
zucchini, pumpkins dusted by the fine ash of fall,
the old riverboat's calliope plays for her,
holds her yearning in audio ecstasy—
sings along the icy well-rope's taut design.
She rocks, or works, and takes
the treasures into her lap, cradling
huge beaming tomatoes
as if they were lost babes.
Her voice quavers. She laughs so glad.
Suddenly she is sure.
She loves her daughter well,
being one, having been one, herself.

PORTAL

We think we learn and mature—
but this is only an illusion,
maya, veil dropped
across our senses.

What you wish for
will happen,
what you state
will form.

There was a wildness in her—
a streak   of madness. Her visceral
being galloping   out of control
gasping and freefall-writhing
for air—

To make a poem form
under the rocks

and grow like a radish.

The child knew.

Various, the images
the blowing bag twists
dances in the wind
tumbling before   the rolling automobile
the crumpled brown paper
forever altered

behind our eyelids
an after thought
lasting   a moment or two

after looking at
the man who was beloved,
the job worked
for ten long years.

~

Bags blow in the street.
Don't drive over them. You
don't know what's in them.
You never know.
It could be a tiny body
or a bomb
splintering through the rubber
of your tires.

Under the table
smoking embers
It's already started—
a fire.

When I was a child
I read an article
in *True* magazine
about people who burst
into flame
Not a racehorse straining
after glory with bursting heart,
but flaming blue workshirts,
the black and white uniforms
of maids on fire—
flesh as combustible
as air.

Is it only sentiment?

In *The Tempest*, like the id,
'such stuff as dreams are made of'
we exaggerate, demonstrate,
our wills fuel the show, draw
futures larger than life—
Yet the mind cut from the body
is labyrinth

And I have been influenced by the voices
of my generation
fragmented, in pieces,
whining in the tin ear of history—

~

like bones rattling in a cup,
like luck,
like the worst day you
ever had—

I will follow you
and watch the flames

a shadow blowing . . .
shimmering
A prescient mirage in

the now-of-now;
pushing back—
a firm, cool hand

against the wall of time
a white line ever lengthening,
the breath of the desert horizon

America
pushing forever
to stay the same

like an orgasm
we hold ourselves against—
if we bolt, if our will fails
before the thrill, the power—

the door to heaven will close.

LAMENT

There are reasons my heart
burns that you will never
understand: the rose
brushing the ribs of my
sweater, the thin
lines under your throat. O you
with the cap, you with the eager
moustache, lover of your wife; this

is the common meeting ground; this
is where we stand together, alone.

Look you fragile
Males, I miss you. I miss your thoughts
singing through the mirror of night and I
say, what does this have to do with me?

Where *is* this ground?

THE NEW START

The new start is almost here
and when I see you the joys
will be in different clothes.
But you will feel that melting of
hearts all over again, that
compassion like a transfusion,
the red blood a delight. Fresh
as bedsheets, I will eat
your lips, delicate sardines.
Do not be afraid. I never
keep fireflies in jars.
The griefman has gone.
He cannot see you
in my house. He cannot
pierce the hum.